SCHIRMER'S LIBRARY
OF MUSICAL CLASSICS

A. DANNHÄUSER

Solfège des Solfèges

Translated by

J. H. CORNELL

IN THREE BOOKS

Book I — Library Vol. 1289

Book II — Library Vol. 1290

➤ Book III — Library Vol. 1291

G. SCHIRMER, Inc.

DISTRIBUTED BY

HAL•LEONARD®
CORPORATION
7777 W. BLUEMOUND RD. P.O. BOX 13819 MILWAUKEE, WI 53213

Andantino.(♪ = 116)

G. C.*)

*)The initials set at the head of each piece indicate the author's name:— Rod., Rodolphe; H.L.,
Henri Lemoine; G. C., G. Carulli; Schnei., Schneitzhoeffer.

4

LEO.

2.

6

Andantino.($\bullet$. = 48)

ROD.

mf

cre-

scen   do   f

Allegro moderato. (♩ = 96)

H.L.

10.

f

mf   sf

p   p

mf   f   mf

f   p   p

poco riten.

f a tempo.   p

p   sf

Andante giusto. (= 72)

RIGHINI.

11.

12

Cantabile.(♩ = 92)   SACCHINI.

12.

Lessons on changing clefs, with the G-clef and F-clef.

Moderato. (♩ = 88)

ROD.

Andantino.(♪ = 104)

D. ALBERTI.

14.

Andante moderato.(♩ = 69)   SCHNEI.

15.

Moderato. (♩ = 108)

18.

The C-clef on the First Line,

employed for the Soprano Voice.

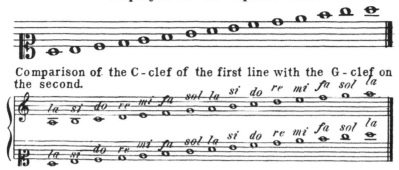

Comparison of the C-clef of the first line with the G-clef on the second.

Exercises within the compass of the Soprano Voice.

Let the pupil name the notes, and afterwards sol-fa them if it be judged necessary. In this case let a measure of two beats be beaten to each note.

Andante grazioso. (♩ = 58)

H.L.

33.

Allegro deciso.($\d = 96$)

ROD.

34.

Allegro moderato.(♩= 108)

35.

più dolce.

Lessons on changing clefs, with the G - clef, the F-clef, and the C-clef on the first line.

cre - -scen - -do

f

dolce.

Largo. (♩ = 78)   N. CONFORTO.

38.

mf sostenuto.

Andantino con espress. (♩ = 80)

J. C. BACH.

39.

Allegro moderato. (♩ = 100)

G.C.

46.

Moderato. (♩ = 63)

A. SCARLATTI.

41.

Andante.(♩.= 50) SCHNEI.

42.

p e ben egualmente.

cresc.

The C-clef, on the Third Line,

employed for the Contralto Voice, the Alto Trombone, and the Tenor Violin.

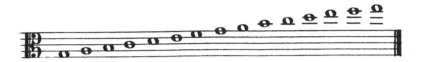

Comparison of the C-clef on the third line with the G-clef on the second.

Exercises within the compass of the Soprano Voice.

Let the pupil name the notes and afterwards sol-fa them if it be judged necessary. In this case, let a measure of two beats be beaten to each note.

42

44

Andante. (♩.= 48)

49.

Moderato. (♩ = 69)

SCHNEI.

50.

dimin. e rallent.

46

PORPORA.

51.

Lessons on changing clefs, with the G-clef, the F-clef, and the C-clefs
on the first and third lines.

DURANTE.

52.

48

Moderato. (♩ = 138)   CAFFARO.

55.

52

Allegro moderato. (♩.= 92)

SCHNEI.

56.

The C-clef, on the Fourth Line,

employed for the Tenor Voice, the Bassoon, the Tenor Trombone, and the Violoncello.

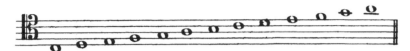

Notes in the G-clef corresponding to those in the C clef on the fourth line.

Exercises within the compass of the Soprano Voice.*

Let the pupil name the notes, and afterwards sol-fa them if it be judged necessary. In this case, let a measure of two beats be beaten to each note.

* Soprano or contralto voices (of women or children) which have to execute music written in the C-clef on the fourth line, sing the tones an octave higher than their actual notation.

54

58

Andantino. (♩= 58)

63.

LEO.

Vivace. (♩ = 126)

DURANTE.

64.

Lessons in changing clefs, with the G-clef, the F-clef, and the C-clefs on the first, third, and fourth lines.

SCHIRMER'S LIBRARY
of Musical Classics
SONG COLLECTIONS

The Library Volume Number is given in brackets: [1363]

ALBUM OF SACRED SONGS. A Collection of 22 Favorite Songs suitable for use in the churches.
High [1384]; Low [1385]

ANTHOLOGY OF ITALIAN SONG OF THE 17TH AND 18TH CENTURIES. 59 Songs. i. e.
Book I [290]; Book II [291]

BEETHOVEN, L. VAN
AN DIE FERNE GELIEBTE (To the Distant Beloved) A cycle of 6 songs. Op. 98. g. e. High [616]; Low [617]
SIX SONGS. g. e. High [618]; Low [619]

BRAHMS, J.
FIFTY SELECTED SONGS. g. e. Low [1581]; High [1582]

CHOPIN, F.
SEVENTEEN POLISH SONGS. Op. 74. g. e. High [249]; Low [250]

FIELITZ, A. VON
ELILAND. A cycle of 10 songs. Op. 9. g. e. Medium [694]; High [695]

FOSTER, S. C.
ALBUM OF SONGS. 20 Favorite Compositions. Collected and edited by H. V. Milligan [1439]

FRANZ, R.
VOCAL ALBUM. 62 Songs. g. e. High [1572]; Low [1573]

GRIEG, E.
SELECTED SONGS. g. e. High [1592]; Low [1593]

LISZT, F.
TWELVE SONGS. g. or f. & e. Low [1613]; High [1614]

MENDELSSOHN, F.
SIXTEEN SELECTED SONGS. g. e. Low [1644]; High [1645]
SIXTEEN TWO-PART SONGS. g. e. [377]

SCHUBERT, F.
FIRST VOCAL ALBUM (3 Cycles, and 24 Favorite Songs). g. e. High [342]; Low [343]
THE MAID OF THE MILL (Die schöne Müllerin) A cycle of 20 songs. g. e. High [344]; Low [345]
WINTER-JOURNEY (Die Winterreise) A cycle of 24 songs. g. e. High [346]; Low [347]
TWENTY-FOUR FAVORITE SONGS. g. e. High [350]; Low [351]
SECOND VOCAL ALBUM. 82 Songs. g. e. [352]

SCHUMANN, R.
VOCAL ALBUM. 55 Songs. g. e. High [120]; Low [121]
WOMAN'S LIFE AND LOVE (Frauenliebe und -leben) A cycle of 8 songs. g. e. High [1356]; Low [1357]

TCHAIKOVSKY, P. I.
TWELVE SONGS. g. e. Low [1620]; High [1621]

WAGNER, R.
FIVE SONGS. g. e. Low [1181]; High [1233]

(Languages of texts are shown in small letters: e. = English; f. = French; g. = German;
i. = Italian. Where there is no other indication, texts are in English only.)

G. SCHIRMER, Inc.

DISTRIBUTED BY

HAL•LEONARD® CORPORATION